Inside-Out Selling
Forget Technique, Know Your Customer

Inside-Out Selling
Craig Klein

Published in 2016 Craig Klein
Houston, Texas
On the web: http://www.salesnexus.com

Please send errors to info@salesnexus.com

Publisher: Craig Klein
Copyright © 2016 Craig Klein

All rights reserved. No part of this publication may be reproduced or transmitted in any form or by any means, electronic or mechanical, including photocopy, recording or any information storage and retrieval system, without prior permission in writing from the publisher.

Table of Contents

Introduction 1
Finding Your Mission In Life 3
Organization - Daily, Weekly, Monthly Goals 7
Understanding the Buying Process 11
Buyers are Liars (why buyers lie, and how to deal with it) 19
Consultative Selling, Listening 23
Empathy 27
Compliments are Key 31
Phone Selling 39
Funnel Math 45
From Ideas to Practice 51
About the Author 53
Special Offer 55

Introduction

How do you train a salesperson? How do you train a salesperson to be successful? These questions are not new. However, with the radical changes wrought by technology on all things related to marketing and selling, the difference between success and failure can be razor thin. Traditional sales training focuses on technique when talking with customers but, one of the greatest challenges today is to get that conversation started.

What follows is what I feel is essential to succeed in sales today. We're not going to rehash old approaches to basic selling. There is a lot available in books, courses and online to teach salespeople to cold call, write emails and give presentations, etc.

What I see every day is sales managers and sales people that know the basics but, struggle to pull it all together into a winning sales strategy. Often, they're working very hard and using great technique. However, they often are applying their sales skills in the wrong place at the wrong time. Many sales organizations are operating on assumptions that were accurate 15 years ago but, are completely wrong today.

We've tried to combine very high level concepts, strategies and frameworks that are the essential structure of a successful sales strategy in today's world with some specific examples and exercises to help you practice and gauge your skill level.

This book should give you a roadmap of areas where you are doing great, areas where minor adjustments might be helpful and areas where you may need additional training or outside help.

What I know from my 25 years of leading salespeople is that there is no quota busting, top producing salesperson on the face of the planet that has not mastered all of these skills and techniques.

Here's to your success!

Finding Your Mission In Life

I've seen a lot of salespeople that show up and work hard for a period of time and then seem to run out of steam. Maybe they get bored, or maybe they have distractions outside of work, whatever. If I'm going to invest weeks and months in a salesperson's development, I want to know why they want to succeed and what really drives them.

Some can tell you about their life plans and goals instantly and some really haven't put much thought into it. The best way to know to motivate people is to help them get where they're going. Helping them answer this question for themselves is essential to long term success and can build an incredible bond between salesperson and manager.

To help your salesperson identify their driving motivation, here are some helpful questions to ask:

- "When you're on your deathbed and your dearest friends and family are around you, who do you want them to see? The person who has accomplished what? ...participated in what? ...treated people how? ...acquired or built what?.
- What do you want to have achieved personally and professionally in your life?
- Where do you want to be in 10 years?

Especially for salespeople, the initial answers to these types of questions often times tend to be mostly material. There needs to be some attention paid to what they can give back to the universe.

Motivation - long term vision and goals

Map out a timeline for their goals.

- When?
- Who will be involved?
- What resources are required?
- Where will the resources come from?
- How will we get the resources?
- How will you know when those goals have been achieved?

Making plans to reach those goals is a huge key. A goal with no plan is a dream, a fantasy. A goal with a plan is a reality on its way to arriving.

This is one area where things tend to get very financially focused very quickly. It's important to try and de-emphasize the financial aspects, especially in the early phases of the plan. Focus on the specific actions that will be performed each day, week month, year, etc. In the same way, the "giving back" elements have a tendency to be far off in the future…. "Once I'm rich, I'll start a charitable foundation!…" I think it's important to find ways to put charitable or altruistic goals on the near term plan. This develops a muscle that many sales people just don't have. Of course, it's also just plain rewarding and has a huge impact on empathy, which we'll get to later.

Exercise

Ask your sales team to write down the answers to these questions individually. A great team building exercise can be to share their answers to these questions with each other, or you can just review it with them and discuss it.

<u>Questions to Ask to Define Long Term Personal Goals</u>

1. What do you or have your enjoyed doing most?
2. What activities do you get "lost" in?
3. What makes you feel great about yourself?

4. Who inspires you most? (Anyone you know or do not know. Family, friends, authors, artists, leaders, etc.) Which qualities inspire you, in each person?
5. What are you naturally good at? (Skills, abilities, gifts etc.)
6. What do people typically ask you to help them with?
7. What would you teach if asked?
8. What would you regret not doing, being or having in your life?
9. You are now 90 years old, sitting on a rocking chair outside your porch; you can feel the spring breeze gently brushing against your face. You are blissful and happy, and are pleased with the wonderful life you've been blessed with. Looking back at your life and all that you've achieved and acquired, all the relationships you've developed; what matters to you most? List them out.
10. What are your deepest values?
11. Select 3 to 6 "value words"[1] and prioritize the words in order of importance to you.
12. What were some challenges, or obstacles you've overcome or are in the process of overcoming? How did you manage to accomplish that?
13. What causes do you strongly believe in? Connect with?
14. If you could get a message across to a large group of people, what would your message be? Who would you want the message to be heard by?
15. How could you use your talents, passions and values to serve, to help and/or to contribute to people, beings, causes, organizations, the planet, etc?

Create Your Personal Mission Statement

Once the questions above, ask each salesperson to take time to write a personal mission statement as below. Then have them share their mission statement with the rest of the team as a group.

---

1   https://salesnexus.com/blog/example-value-words/

- List out actions words you connect with.
  - Example: educate, accomplish, empower, encourage, improve, help, give, guide, inspire, integrate, master, motivate, nurture, organize, produce, promote, travel, spread, share, satisfy, understand, teach, write, etc.
- Based on your answers to the 15 questions, list everything and everyone that you believe you can help.
  - Example: People, creatures, organizations, causes, groups, environment, etc.
- Identify your end goal. How will the '**who**' from your above answer benefit from what you '**do**'?
- Combine these steps into 1-3 sentences.

Organization - Daily, Weekly, Monthly Goals

Anyone that's managed salespeople know that basic organization skills are essential to a salesperson, and are often quite a weak spot. Combined with the goals and action plans above, good organization skills are like a knife in the hands of a good chef.

Learning to block out windows of time in your day for important activities is crucial. Learning to put the most important at the top of the list, early in the day avoids procrastination.

Learning to set goals for very granular, but essential tasks is an absolute must. Not just setting goals, but quantifying how to achieve those goals is key.

- "I will knock on 20 doors this morning."
- "I will call 50 new prospects this week."
- "I will research and find 10 new strategic accounts to target this week."

With the personal mission statement from the preceding chapter as the foundation, even these mundane goals can be tied to a long term vision of success and happiness.

Exercise

<u>Annual Goal</u>

>Ask yourself: What would you like to be able to say about yourself, your career, your happiness in one year?

>Complete this sentence: "This year has been a huge success for me because I…."

<u>6 Month Goal</u>

>What do you need to accomplish within the first 6 months in order to accomplish your annual goal?

>What actions must be undertaken?

>Whose help will I need?

>Likely or possible obstacles?

>Personal investment? What percentage of my time should I devote? Money? Travel? Less time with family or involved in other important activities?

>How will I measure my progress?

>How can I reward myself for taking these actions?

<u>3 Month Goal</u>

>What do you need to accomplish within the first 3 months in order to accomplish your 6 month goal?

>What actions must be undertaken?

>Whose help will I need?

>Likely or possible obstacles?

>Personal investment? What percentage of my time should I devote? Money? Travel? Less time with family or involved in other important activities?

How will I measure my progress?

How can I reward myself for taking these actions?

<u>1 Month Goal</u>

What do you need to accomplish within the first 1 month in order to accomplish your 3 month goal?

What actions must be undertaken?

Whose help will I need?

Likely or possible obstacles?

Personal investment? What percentage of my time should I devote? Money? Travel? Less time with family or involved in other important activities?

How will I measure my progress?

How can I reward myself for taking these actions?

Understanding the Buying Process

What makes someone buy something? It's not because they saw an awesome presentation, it's because they have a need or a problem that is affecting them on an emotional level. Even in business situations, people buy for emotional reasons.

We all have pretty basic emotional needs, and in the end, every purchase can be tied back to satisfying one or more of those needs. The business reasons for the purchase are just the rationalization of that emotional need. The technical reasons are just another way of rationalizing the need.

"Why did you buy those expensive new headphones?", she asks me. "Because I'm editing all of this audio for our Youtube videos and those cheap ones didn't have the frequency range to let me filter out the static properly.", I say. When the real truth is that I have been watching Youtube videos about how to make awesome, professional videos and the "experts" all use these expensive headphones and I want to feel like and look like an expert.

Buying Phases

Many buyers cannot identify the real emotional reasons they're making a purchase themselves because, they are not always conscious of it. This is why typical television advertising works so well. I want to feel and look like the people I see in the ad so I buy the weight loss product whose name you mention at the end.

Salespeople can best maximize their opportunity by developing a keen sense of where the buyer is in the process.

The buyer may not be able to say that they're unhappy with their job and would like a trip to Vegas to blow off steam, but, when presented with an opportunity to do just that, which can be rationalized as making an investment in marketing at a trade show, they might move mountains to make it happen.

Most B2B sales discussions never touch on the emotional aspects. It can be perceived as inappropriate in a professional setting. There may be more than one person influencing the decision, and they'll each have their own emotions of course. Typically, the conversation centers on the business and technical rationalizations for the purchase.

Every buying process goes through the exact same phases that may be at an emotional, business, or technical level (or all three).

- **Awareness** - the customer first becomes aware of an opportunity, need or problem.
- **Action** - the customer decides to do something about it.
- **Research** - the customer absorbs information about causes of the problem, and possible options/solutions., etc. Here they are primarily accumulating enough knowledge to confirm that they have a clear understanding of the problem or opportunity and the range of possible options/solutions.
- **Engagement** - the customer starts to take action with one or more solution provider - filling out a form on the site, calling sales, contacting support, downloading a report, etc. Here they are beginning to consider specific solutions - options, pricing, terms, etc.
- **Purchase** - the customer at least thinks they know what they want to buy, may attempt to negotiate and may or may not actually make the purchase.

<u>Here's a breakdown of the emotional state of the buyer, and "do's"/"don'ts" for each phase:</u>

Awareness

Emotional State: Emotions high. Possibly scared or excited. Possibly not all that rational.

Don't: Offer solutions. Quote prices. Be Aggressive. Start talking about yourself. Don't fix.

Do: Be empathetic. Ask open ended questions. Get them talking about the story behind the situation. Keep the focus of the conversation on them. Help them process this new situation by listening. Use validating statements - "That must have been tough." "I bet that made you angry." "Were you scared?" "How did you feel about that?" "Tell me more about that." Keeping them talking by using open ended questions helps keep them engaged and increases the opportunity of moving the conversation to the next stages. Keeping them talking is a great sign that the conversation is moving forward . Always use open ended questions, Not Yes or No questions.

Magic ingredient: When you find yourself in a conversation like this, stay there!. The salesperson's instinct is to try and move things forward. However, listening and validating the customer's feelings is the most powerful exercise in building trust available. Let the customer decide when it's time to move on. When they say "So, I guess I need to do something about this.", the salesperson can say, "Maybe but, I can tell this is scary/upsetting/emotional for you. Are you sure you don't want to take some time to process this?" Or "I think I might be able to help but, I'm so grateful that you've shared your story with me. Thank you! When you're ready, I might have some suggestions we could discuss." Keeping the ball in their court gives them reassurance and increases the chance of gaining their trust.

Action

Emotional State: Resolved. Curious. Possibly jumping to conclusions.

Don't: Jump to the purchase phase! Suggest solutions, and. Tell them what they should do.

Do: Help them rationalize the potential purchase and. Help them envision themselves in the future once the solution is in place. Ask questions like "What will you do with your time once this is over/fixed?" "How will you feel once this is all over?" Help them envision the realistic decision making process - "Who else will be involved in making this kind of change?" "Do you think they see the problem the way you do?"

Magic Ingredient: Remember that they have only just realized a need and decided to take action. They're still processing all of this. To build trust, let them be in control of the pace of the process. Don't offer a solution yet. Help them begin researching options. "Thank you for sharing. Would you mind if I shared a few stories/case studies of how customers with similar concerns addressed this issue?"

Research

Emotional State: Investigative. Inquisitive. Questioning.

Don't: Quote prices. Provide spec sheets or brochures or contracts. Get defensive if they're investigating options that aren't in your sweet spot.

Do: Tell stories about other customers. Share case studies. Provide educational materials. Share informative but neutral content (not sales pitches or brochures).

Magic Ingredient: The buyer's instinct is to tell salespeople to leave them alone until they've done their research. "We're looking into all our options and putting our requirements together. Once we've done, I'll let you know when we're ready for a proposal." The only way to stay engaged with the customer is to been seen as a resource for unbiased information and learning. Create one or two crucial resources that fit the bill - 5 Key Questions to Ask Vendors When Buying a ????.

Engagement

Emotional State: Ready to talk. Open to discussions, meetings, presentations, etc. Coordinating. Accommodating.

Don't: Jump to Closing or Asking for the Order.

Do: Help them be sure they've thought of everything and are being thorough. Ask for written requirements docs, and offer to help them document the requirements. Revisit who's involved in the decision. Ask about budget authority.

Magic Ingredient: Many customers have worked themselves through all the above phases and "appear" to the salesperson at this phase. It's crucial to establish trust quickly as you can assume that the buyer is "engaging" with more than one vendor simultaneously. Help them be sure they're ready to make a purchase. Go back to the beginning and ask the "why" questions. "You're ready to set up a demo? Great! Since this is our first time to talk, I want to be sure you get whatever best fits your unique needs. From your perspective, what is the core reason you're making this investment?" "Have you made a written list of requirements?" "Have you made this type of purchase before?" "Have you researched how similar customers have addressed this problem?" "Tell me about your research and decision making process that led you to me." Offer resources from the above phases where applicable.

Purchase

Emotional State: Get it done mode. Open and honest. Negotiating.

Don't: Assume you're the only vendor they're having this conversation with. Buyers often "pretend" to be in buying mode when they're not. Don't assume the person you're talking with has the sole authority to execute the purchase.

Do: Qualify their readiness to make the purchase. "When do you need to have this up and running/in place/delivered?" "Are there others that need to be part of this decision?" "Are you still considering other vendors/solutions?" "Who will be involved in the implementation? What's their availability for this project?"

Magic Ingredient: The greatest problem that undermines salespeople and businesses trying to forecast sales is customers that pretend to be ready to buy when they're not. There are many reasons for this, (more on that later) but, essentially, they're trying to avoid sales pitches and get pricing and specs from an overeager salesperson. Really, they're at the Research stage. Be skeptical about customers that appear out of nowhere ready for quotes and proposals. They may have already decided to go with a competitor and are using you to get competing quotes for negotiation purposes. If you haven't had the conversations that are elicited by all the questions in the previous phases, then start them immediately. Start asking questions about why, who, when, etc. If they are genuine, this will be how you become their trusted advisor while all your competitors appear to care about nothing but their money. If they are "pretending", they'll appreciate your thoroughness unless they are already in bed with another vendor.

Exercise

Make a list of the things that "trigger" a need for your products and services in your customers.

- What are the events that commonly occur in their life that cause them to suddenly realize a need for your product?
- What are the incidents that come up that cause them to become frustrated with their current vendor?

If you target separate market segments or demographics, make a separate list of triggers for each group.

These are the questions you can ask new prospects to determine how urgent their need is and where they are in their own process.

What are the actions these different types of customers will take as they enter each of the buying stages described above?

When you're typical customer starts the research phase, what places will they begin looking? Are their industry or educational resources that are commonly called upon by your customers?

Create a map of these "triggers" for each segment or audience or market.

Example:

	Food Services	**Hospitals**	**Airlines**
Awareness	Food waste, spoiled food	Patient complaints	Poor customer ratings
Action	Begin contacting vendors	Brought up at board meeting	Convene a committee to research solutions
Research	Talk with other regions, restaurants	Bring in consultant	Purchase studies
Engagement	Concerned about costs/budget	Requirements defined, time to find a vendor	Trying to combine with menu update
Purchase	Ready to make the change	In next year's budget	Rollout date targeted

These triggers can each be the basis of very effective content marketing. Articles, emails and webinars on these topics will attract customers at that stage in their buying process. This type of marketing content or collateral can also help to move customers forward in their own process.

Drill salespeople on these triggers. "Customer calls in and says, 'We've been talking with other restaurants about how they manage food spoilage'. What stage are they in?"

What are their likely concerns at each stage? How can I help them feel educated, comfortable or confident about those concerns?

Buyers are Liars (why buyers lie, and how to deal with it)

It's easy for salespeople to see themselves as the conduit for all information. It's almost impossible for a salesperson to fully appreciate how much information the customer is presented with online and how that "colors" their perspective.

Retargeting is a relatively new trend that has tremendous ability to skew the customer's perspective. Essentially, when a customer visits your competitor's site, they begin to see the competitor's ads showing up on completely unrelated websites they visit. So, I visit a plumber's website and later, at home, I'm researching vacation spots and that plumber's ads are showing up.

Even a salesperson making outbound calls needs to be aware of the experience a buyer will have online as they research options and solutions and your brand. In traditional sales approaches, the salesperson is essentially the catalyst for the entire process. The customer is happily going about their business when they receive a call from a salesperson that asks questions that help them become aware that they have a problem or need. Then they begin their own research process, after they finish the call with the salesperson. What will they find?

In a business spending money on digital marketing, content marketing and generating "inbound" leads, often the process is designed so that the buyer goes from Awareness all the way to the Purchase phase online, without any interaction with sales. So, the salesperson can easily fall into the habit of assuming the customer has checked off all the other boxes. As mentioned earlier, that can be a big mistake.

It's a good idea to ask questions about the process overall. "How did you find us?" "What other solutions are you looking at?" If there are comparison or buyer's guides published by neutral parties put your product or service in a good light, it's great to suggest those. Offering objective resources like this builds trust. "Have you purchased something like this before?" "Tell me about that experience?" "What worked?" "What didn't work?" "What would you do differently?" "How long have you been researching solutions to this problem?"

Bottom line: Buyers will have a tendency to make it seem as if yours is the first brand they've looked at and the one they are primarily interested in. And salespeople will have a tendency to assume it and believe it. So, develop a reflex to take a step backwards. As they say, "When it seems too good to be true, it probably is."

In many businesses, the primary goal of the initial conversation with a prospect is to "disqualify" the prospect if possible. The salesperson's time is very valuable to themselves and to the organization. Wasting time on prospects that are not ready to buy is to be avoided at all costs.

Define what makes a customer a "hot one". Ask questions to identify those traits in every prospect and focus time on those that are most qualified. Develop systems and processes to nurture those that are unqualified.

Download a handy printout[2] for any salesperson to put on the wall to keep empathetic questions, qualifying and letting go of disqualified prospects "top of mind".

---

2   https://salesnexus.com/blog/wp-content/uploads/2016/12/Inside-Out-Selling-Reminders.pdf

Exercise

Pick an innocuous topic and question each other about it, purposely lying. See if you can spot the "tells" below…

Verbal signs a person is lying:

> Qualifiers: not necessarily, but, however, almost, basically.
>
> Denials of lying: frankly, obviously, to be 100% honest with you, as far as I know.
>
> Speech errors: this is the old Freudian slip, changing your thoughts and details mid-stream. Pause-fillers: filling empty spaces with um, er, ah, uh.
>
> Stuttering: a liar gets tongue-tied, runs words together, stammers and slurs his speech.

Nonverbal signs of lying:

> Lip licking
>
> Lip puckering
>
> Increased drinking and swallowing
>
> Hand-to-face
>
> Sighs/deep breaths
>
> Hand and shoulder shrugs
>
> Handling objects
>
> Looking away to the side or down
>
> Crossing arms
>
> Closing hands into fists

Consultative Selling, Listening

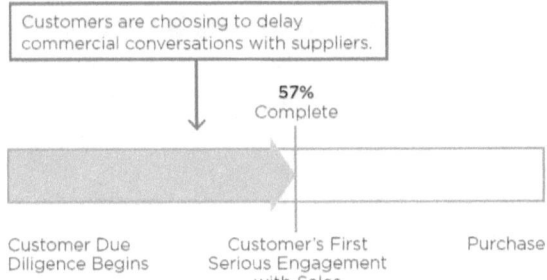

Figure 1: Degree of Progress Through the Purchase Process Before Engaging Sales
Customer Average

Selling in the Internet age is not what it was before everything you ever wanted to know was available with few keystrokes. The salesperson's primary role was to be the provider of information by walking prospects through options, explaining them, etc.

Today, prospects get all of that information online before they ever talk to a salesperson. In general, customers perceive salespeople as difficult to deal with and untrustworthy. So, they avoid contacting sales until they have no choice. See the image above and this Forbes article[3] - Customers are 57% through the buying process before they engage sales!

So what is the role of the salesperson? **Let's start by discussing what doesn't work.**

DON'T:

- Educate too much. The customer is likely already informed.
- Spend too much time doing presentations.
- Assume you know what the customer needs.

---

3   http://www.forbes.com/sites/gyro/2013/01/07/the-disappearing-sales-process/#237d403125d9

Given that the customer is already highly informed before talking to a salesperson, salespeople should be cautious about doing too much "telling" or educating at all. Customers generally have specific questions. Find out what those are and provide clear, concise answers with lots of backup materials on your website.

In the same vein, salespeople should spend bunches of time doing presentations. That sort of content can easily be recorded and available on your website, saving both the customer and your team time.

In complex sales situations where the salesperson is reaching out to customers that are not already shopping, the objective of the salesperson is to identify the need of the customer that can be addressed and to help the customer appreciate the value of addressing that need. Salespeople take on the role of consultant or even counselor. Have you ever had someone that thought they were really smart show up and tell you what you ought to do? How did that make you feel? How did you respond?

Salespeople should not assume they know what the customer needs. No one ever bought anything because someone told them they should. Each customer has to go through their own mental process of recognizing a need, decided to act on the need, considering options and making decisions. The salesperson's role is to help the customer through that voyage. Remember that the customer can and probably is visiting multiple competitors' websites. They're going to spend time with the salespeople they like.

Of course, the overabundance of information online can be overwhelming and confusing. Prospects often need assurance that the solution really is the right fit. They want to tell someone they trust about their specific situation to see what the best options are for them.

Think of the people you trust the most in life. Is it because they're always telling you what you need to know or what you ought to do? Probably not. Consulting for Dummies summarizes effective consulting as:[4]

---

[4] http://www.dummies.com/how-to/content/consulting-skill-listening-to-a-potential-client.html

- Asking open ended questions
- Using active silence
- Asking clarifying questions
- Confirming Understanding

If a salesperson asks a prospect, "Why have you decided to change your power provider?" and the response is along the lines of "It's just time for a change." or "We're just tired of those guys." without elaboration, the salesperson's best friend is silence. Instead of instantly responding to a short, "avoidance" response like that, the salesperson can just calmly pause, maintaining eye contact if in person or just being perfectly quiet if on the phone, and wait for the customer to dig deeper.

The salesperson must have an innate sense of when they've learned enough about a given subject from the customer so they'll know when they need to dig deeper and when it's time to move onto another subject.

Practicing deepening questions can be very powerful. Here are some good "deepening questions" that can push the customer to share the deeper emotional reasons that a change is called for:

- "Tell me more about that…"
- "How did that make you feel?"
- "What did you do about that?",

Remember, a key goal is to establish trust. There are two old adages about sales and buyers that still hold true:

> **"People buy from people they like."**
> **"People buy for emotional reasons."**

Here is an example of an effective conversation between a customer and a salesperson:

(Customer): "I've decided to buy a new air compressor. I've been on your website and I want to get the model AXJ5000."

(Salesperson): "Oh, that's great! There is a lot of great info about that model on our site and I'm glad you've taken the time to investigate.

However, it's my job to make absolutely sure that you get the best fit for your needs on the best possible terms. Do you mind if I ask you a few questions to understand what exactly you need?"

That response helps the customer trust. There is a little voice in the customer's mind saying, "Hmm… this guy seems to really care. I like that!".

Often, it's helpful to construct very detailed "personas" that the salesperson can use in identifying customers' needs and knowing if more questions are needed or it's time to move on.

Identify the most common types of buyers and their typical traits.

- What's their education level, income, age, marital status?
- What's the application of the product?
- What are the unique advantages of your offering that are most meaningful to this buyer?

Remember, people buy for emotional reasons so, generally, you want to continue digging deeper until you hear the customer talking about emotional and personal things rather than technical and business circumstances.

Exercise

Questions, No Statements - engage in conversations amongst yourselves with the following rules: One Listener, One Answerer; The Listener can only ask questions, no statements except you can only say those that are requests for more information… "tell me more about that"

Interruption - In team meetings, choose a "scorekeeper" to tally up the number of times each team member interrupts another. Reward the members with the least interruptions. Give an undesired task to those with the most interruptions.

Repeat It - Ask questions of each other. When the answer is finished, have the listener or questioner repeat back what they heard trying to be as detailed as possible.

Empathy

What is more valuable to the customer - your advice, or your empathy/listening? This is crucial for salespeople to grasp. The most effective form of persuasion is not "convincing" the customer of anything, it is helping the customer to reach their own conclusion.

A customer that is asked to listen to a lot of explanation of features and benefits will tune out eventually or possibly even be irritated. A customer who is asked genuine questions of curiosity and interest will be deeply engaged and will eventually "see the light" themselves.

Exercise: Just Like Me

Before a meeting with a customer or even a phone call, try this "meditation" from Search Inside Yourself.[5] This will focus you on asking questions from an empathetic point of view and searching for what really benefits the customer the most.

Read the words below slowly to yourself, pausing to reflect at the end of each sentence:

> *This person has a body and a mind, just like me.*
>
> *This person has feelings, emotions, and thoughts, just like me.*
>
> *This person has, at some point in his or her life, been sad, disappointed, angry, hurt or confused, just like me.*

---

5   https://siyli.org/

This person has, in his or her life, experienced physical and emotional pain and suffering, just like me.

This person wishes to be free from pain and suffering, just like me.

This person wishes to be healthy and loved, and to have fulfilling relationships, just like me.

This person wishes to be happy, just like me.

Then allow some wishes for this person to arise by reading the following:

I wish for this person to have the strength, the resources, and the emotional and social support to navigate the difficulties in life.

I wish for this person to be free from pain and suffering.

I wish for this person to be happy.

Because this person is a fellow human being, just like me.

Now, I wish for everybody I know to be happy.

Download a handy printout[6] for any salesperson to put on the wall to keep empathetic questions, qualifying and letting go of disqualified prospects "top of mind".

Exercise: Process Praise

When meeting a customer, notice things about them. What kind of car did they drive up in? Where did they go to school? What hobbies do they have?

Then, rather than pointing out those obvious "traits", find ways to praise what they did to accomplish or acquire those things.

Instead of "Oh, I see you went to State College, I love their football team!", say "Wow! You went to State College, I bet you had to work hard to get admitted!" or "and you got your degree in Nuclear Physics, that must have been incredibly difficult!"

---

6   https://salesnexus.com/blog/wp-content/uploads/2016/12/Inside-Out-Selling-Reminders.pdf

Exercise: Self Assessment

After a meeting or conversation, ask yourself the following questions to assess if you did a good job of really understanding the customer.

1. Can you identify the currently held belief of the customer that you must convince them to change?
2. How will that change benefit them specifically?
3. What feelings do they have that are making them resist the change?
4. What are they afraid of?

If you don't feel you gained a clear understanding of these answers, write down a few questions that you feel would have led to that understanding. Make sure to ask them in your next meeting!

Compliments are Key

You may seek to achieve purely selfish ends through learning the art of compliments. There is nothing wrong with that. It's my belief that even when our intentions are not admirable, if we practice the art of connecting with people and making them feel better about themselves, good things happen.

The more you practice the art, the greater your reverence for it.

Have you ever heard the phrase "Kill them with kindness"? Have you ever noticed that seemingly insignificant words of praise or encouragement can brighten someone's day?

Of course, we've all experienced this, both as the giver of compliments and as the receiver.

Think back to the earliest time in childhood that you can remember someone saying something really nice to you. "You're so smart!" or "You're so pretty." or even "You're getting so big!" How did that simple comment, that perhaps your grandmother or aunt or neighbor said to all the kids, make you feel? Wonderful! Almost so much that you could feel a warmth inside of you. Like it set your motor running in a higher gear. You could feel their love and also, learned to love yourself just a little bit more.

Unfortunately, this simple and innocent way to connect with others becomes either misused or underused by most adults. Because it can be used as a kind of manipulation, others tend to shy away from giving out compliments for fear of being perceived as Machiavellian.

But, more importantly most of us miss several opportunities every day to truly connect with others in a real and even life changing way.

When we first experience a compliment that truly touches our heart, it opens our eyes to the possibility that we may have special and unique gifts, and that we might be different than everyone else in some important way.

A compliment helps us love ourselves. And isn't that the unfortunate reality of most of human existence? We spend so much of our lives questioning or even doubting ourselves. Life is hard, people can be harsh judges and typically our harshest critic is ourselves.

A friend once told me, when discussing dating, "Tell the pretty ones they're smart and the smart ones they're pretty." And it truly works wonders. You see good looking people hear how good looking they are all the time. Great athletes hear how amazing their talents are all the time. But, that doesn't mean that they don't have insecurities and frailties.

Our doubts about ourselves are what keep us from acting. They keep us in a state of fear. This is a place where our minds can talk us out of just about anything. We miss opportunities and see problems or risks where there really are none.

Most importantly, our insecurities keep us from connecting with other people.

Physicists say that there is no such thing as cold. There is only the absence of heat. The same is true of love. When there is no love, we are left with only our own fears and doubts about ourselves and mistrust of others.

That's why connecting with others is so crucial. Connecting with others is how we transmit love. And compliments are perhaps the simplest and easiest technique we have at our disposal to connect with each other. They cost us nothing and everyone already knows how to do it.

Herein, we'll discuss why we don't employ this powerful tool more often and how the simple act of saying nice things to another can literally change your life.

The Power of Giving Compliments

Compliments open the door to communication and shine light into our internal self esteem, which can often be a dark place. Compliments say you care about someone, that you value them.

Someone that is suffering from challenges you are completely ignorant to can be lifted up by praise of qualities and efforts that have absolutely no relation to their situation.

A compliment can create a feeling of trust and safety that encourages someone to share very intimate and sensitive things with you, creating opportunities to bond very deeply and to help in powerful ways.

Imagine walking into a social event. We've all had the feeling isolation when standing alone with on one to talk to. In that moment, you have to choose who you'll approach to engage in conversation. You look around the room and you see friends, who may already be engaged in conversations, people you don't know who won't make eye contact with you and people who make eye contact with you but, are otherwise engaged. No matter how you view that landscape in that moment, we all have anxiety about approaching others. Compliments are the magic scepter that allow you to successfully approach anyone in the room. A well delivered compliment excuses a complete interruption of another conversation. Just walk up and say "I just had to come over and tell you how much I admire….." No one will resent that interruption.

How to Receive Compliments

It's a testament to the power of compliments that most people aren't very good at receiving them. They're so unfamiliar with the feeling of being complimented that they react with disbelief, embarrassment and denial. "That's an excellent painting Johnny!" is commonly met with "It's not as good as I wanted it to be." or "The colors are not very good."

A compliment is an active attempt to connect. That is such a precious gift! Accept it with grace by recognizing it, not denying it. Just say "Thank you!" Return the favor if you can. But just saying "Thank you! That's so nice of you to say." says to the giver of the compliment that you appreciate it and leaves the door open for more.

Self Love

Praising others is "easy" in terms of the time and physical effort involved. However, it's hard to compliment others when you're not feeling good about yourself. In fact, it's amazing how difficult it can be to say something nice to someone, when your head is full of negative thoughts about yourself.

If you're struggling with complimenting others or maybe someone in particular, then it's probably a sign that there is something going on in your own world that you should look at more closely.

We find it easy to compliment others regarding things we admire ourselves. And we have the highest admiration for things that we aspire to ourselves. So, we recognize those qualities easily in others, we are impressed and are probably comfortable with saying so.

For example, a lady who spent an hour struggling to choose the right dress for a cocktail party sees another lady with a dress she admires and is quick to say "That is such a beautiful dress!". Or a man who's been planning on buying a new car sees someone drive up in a car they're considering and immediately says "Wow! Nice car! How do you like it?"

These are genuine expressions of admiration, and maybe a little bit of envy. They are great! However, these are the least powerful kinds of compliments to give. Why? Because the recipient is probably feeling very confident about their brand new dress or car or whatever.

Complimenting people in areas where they feel least secure is so much more powerful. The real magic of a compliment is when it lifts someone up from a low place.

Are you able to recognize others' insecurities? Often, those things that you are most acutely aware of are also your own deepest insecurities.

And sometimes, the reverse is true. Sometimes we can be blind to others weaknesses or insecurities, because we are so tender and protective of ourselves in those same areas.

Either way, complimenting others has the fringe benefit of allowing us to hold a mirror to ourselves and see our own strengths and weaknesses, greatest confidences and worst insecurities.

One of the greatest sources of insecurity is the way that we all compare what we know about ourselves intimately with what we observe about others. Even a top athlete knows his or her own weaknesses. A basketball star may know they don't have a great free throw percentage, and after a missed free throw costs the team the game, they are likely to be very sensitive about it and probably have a lot of negative "self talk" about their abilities, their work ethic, etc.

Then in the next game, they see a player on the opposing team that wins the game by making almost all of their free throws, and they think to themselves, "I'll never be able to be that good. I'm holding my team back because I can't make free throws. I'll never make it to the pros because I'm not a good free throw shooter."

What this player is doing is comparing one poor performance by himself with one great performance by another. What they don't know is how hard that other player may have to work to be so good at free throws. In basketball, this is a very common weakness. Getting good at free throws normally takes hours and hours of disciplined practice. The kind of practice that's not as fun as playing with friends or teammates, dunking, passing, etc.

We cannot see what others have gone through to achieve or earn what we see them "show up" with. Usually, there is much more sacrifice and struggle than meets the eye.

What separates our current reality from the reality that we want to achieve is usually a bunch of hard work. And we are all very good at saying to ourselves that we don't have the time, talent or resources to achieve those things. Most of the human race is walking through their lives wishing they had certain things and telling themselves that they can't have those things for one reason or another. Maybe you tell yourself you just don't deserve it.

Compliments help us see these things within ourselves. Of course, "fixing" these self-defeating thoughts or overcoming them is not easy or fast. However, one way or another, the bridge between where you are today and where you want to be is built by taking action, one step at a time.

When we notice someone who has achieved something we admire or envy or covet, we can begin to plan our own bridge to the future AND give that person a tremendous compliment by asking them HOW they achieved it.

Rather than admiring the dress or the car, admire the work that went into acquiring it. "That is an awesome car! How in the world could you afford it? You must work very hard!" "I'd love to be able to do that! How did you learn to do it so well?"

If we're good at asking these kind of questions and listening to the stories they elicit, we'll begin to see exactly what we'll have to do to accomplish the same thing. And the more clearly we see the path, the easier the first step will become.

Validation

Compliments give people validation. They say "You're valuable. You're appreciated." We all need validation and drink it up insatiably. All of us have internal thoughts pointing out what's wrong with ourselves and our situation. That's why compliments are so powerful. They are often the opposite of the thoughts we're having internally.

Validating other's worth and importance opens the door to connection and communication. Communication is a challenge in all walks of life. When communication fails, all forms of human endeavor and human happiness begin to fail. Validating others is like the oil that keeps our society growing and running smoothly.

Our ideas are often where we can be most insecure. Validating others' ideas can be incredibly powerful.

We often spend hours mulling over challenges and problems and dreaming of ways to "fix" these problems or of a better world where these challenges don't exist. And this is where many of our ideas come from.

When someone shares an idea with us, they are often sharing something that considerable thought and angst has gone into. It's also often quite a big step to share that idea with others. It can live comfortably in our own mind with no judgement, but exposing it to the judgement of others can be frightening.

Often, when someone shares an idea with us, our first reaction is to judge it not on its own merits but, more in light of our alternative ideas. It's like a competition. If I accept your idea, what does that mean for my idea?

In simple decisions like where to go to lunch, someone has to "win". So, when I'm thinking about a burger and someone suggests Mexican food, my first reaction might be to say "Oh, no! Not Mexican! I can't handle all that cheese!"

What I've just said to that person is "That's a bad idea." I invalidated their idea. When discussing plans and ideas of greater import, this effect can stop connection and communication in its tracks. If you share your idea and I immediately point out its flaws because I have an alternate idea, I've made it difficult for any constructive discussion to take place.

The alternative is not to "accept" others' ideas at the expense of your own but, to validate the ideas of others' first to keep communication flowing and find the win-win compromise.

If he says "I'd like to have Mexican food.", I say "That's a great idea! Thanks for sharing that. I know you love Mexican food," and, I say "I was thinking about having a burger. I'm trying to stay away from too much cheese."

Now there are two ideas on the table with equal value and we can weigh and discuss the merits of both and find a compromise.

Even in a situation where it's not essential to "choose" one idea or solution or to make any decisions, validating the ideas of others can open the doors of human connection in extremely powerful ways.

"I'd like to have a Ferrari someday!" Validate this statement, which you may regard as unrealistic or indulgent or whatever, with "Wow! I love that idea! You dream big!" You'll find that this validation opens the floodgates to more and more inspiring dreams and ideas!

Technique

The first principle of mastering the art of complimenting is to do it. Find something nice to say about as many people as you can. Your grandmother told you this. No matter how seemingly insignificant or obvious or gratuitous, say it. Saying something nice about others says "I care about you, I value you."

Most people spend a tremendous amount of energy trying to appear to others in certain ways. Ladies spend hours primping mostly to impress other ladies. Men flex their muscles to impress other men. The "impressive" traits that are obvious about others can often be a compensation for what they feel are their weaknesses.

Complimenting others in areas that they are not obviously trying to display can be very powerful. A lady who is a striking beauty is probably not used to being complimented on her intelligence and she probably also feels as though it's overlooked.

Choose the "road less traveled" when complimenting others. Praise the things that others are not praising. Look beyond the surface.

Appearance and material possessions are the easy choices. People with obvious strengths will be used to hearing about their strengths and the results or appearance of these strengths. Look for subtleties. Look for the work that went into this strength. Complement the effort or creativity.

The more accomplished and confident the person, the more important it is to look beyond the obvious.

Imagine seeing a celebrity on the street. If you walk up and tell them how much you loved their latest movie, you're just another in a crowd. If you point out what a great parent they seem to be or how you admire their stance on a social issue, you've gotten their attention.

Phone Selling

There has been much written about telephone sales techniques. We won't repeat those lessons, only attempt to highlight certain qualities strategies that are most crucial in today's selling environment.

#1 Phone Mistake - Distraction!

Here's a quote from a great article by Steve Yastrow, Building Customer Relationships by Phone[7] - "Alertness is the most fundamental element of a relationship-building encounter. When you pay attention to every detail of your customer conversation, you will inevitably notice ways to advance the conversation. You wouldn't look at your computer screen if you were sitting face-to-face with a customer, so don't do it when you're on the phone. When you are reading an email from a customer, give it your full attention, discerning exactly what your customer wants to say to you."

The reality is that salespeople have a lots of calls to make and most will end in voicemails so, as they're going through their call list, listening to the phone ring and waiting on hold, they're going to check their email or take a look at the latest sports scores. But, if we're reading an email when the customer answers, it's pretty likely that as the conversation drifts in various directions, we'll find ourselves looking over those emails again, while the customer is still on the phone!

That's bad enough but, guess what… Your customer is doing the exact same thing! Don't assume that when you're explaining the key

---

7   http://yastrow.com/6-tips-building-customer-relationships-phone-email/

differentiation between your product and your competitor's, you have the customer's full attention! You probably don't.

If we maintain full attention on the customer during the conversation, we'll be more effective at hearing the little cues that help us "know" them like we would when we meet with them face to face. And, we'll be much better to maintain the customer's attention.

Stay Focused!

When the conversation starts, close your email program! Turn away from your computer! If you need to review customer information during the conversation, keep that front and center. Discipline yourself to focus only on information related to the conversation at hand.

Ask the "Corny" Questions

Take 10 minutes and make a list of questions you can ask over the phone. That helps you see into the customer's physical world. The things that you would see if you were there... Even the time worn, "corny" ones!

How's the weather? If it's nice, then "Were you able to get out and enjoy it?" "What do you like to do when you get away from the office?" "Did you do anything fun this weekend?" "How many people work in your office?" "Are you in your own office or in a cubical?" "Do you ever work from home?" "Do you have a long commute to work?" "How late do you typically work?" "Do you have kids?" "How old are they?" "What are your plans for the weekend?" "Are you doing any traveling this summer, for the holidays, for spring break, etc.?" "Do you have any photos of your production facility?" "Where did you go to school?" "Where did you grow up?"

Keep your list next to the phone. Make a note of what you learn about each customer. Each time you talk to the customer, ask follow up questions about those personal details. "How did Johnny do in the soccer game?" This is very powerful! It tells the customer that you care and you're listening. These corny questions are no longer just worthless social graces, they're bringing you closer together!

Of course, the best way to keep the customer focused is keep them talking. Ask great questions that make them dig deep.

Give them Something to Look At

If you were in their office, they wouldn't check email in front of you. They'd maintain eye contact with you. Using a webcam meeting tool can accomplish the same thing! Or, just give them resources to look at... "Go to our website and click on..." Build PDFs and webpages that act as visual aids for your conversation. These have the fringe benefit of making sure the customer is more engaged in the conversation.

#2 Mistake - Switching to Email

Here's a great quote from a recent article in Forbes[8] -

> **Be more than an email address.** Despite its prevalence in business today, email communication can often be misconstrued, especially during stressful situations, if senders and recipients do not know each other well. Use other channels to help shed light on who you are. Consider a phone call, Skype or an in-person meeting to put a face (or voice) to a name. Often the phone gets a bad reputation (e.g. using it to 'get on the same page'), but if used for good news, a phone call is a great way to build a better relationship with your client."

So, you've had this awesome first conversation with the customer. She told you all about her kids and the vacation they have planned. She also told you all about the decision making process for purchasing your product! You sent a follow up email to the customer with links to a few things she asked for. All good!

Then, she responded to your email with some additional questions.

You're busy and so is she... So, it's natural to think that it's best for everyone if you just reply to her email. Wrong!

Sure, there may some very technical information that needs to be conveyed via documents, etc. and obviously, an email is a great way

---

[8] http://yastrow.com/6-tips-building-customer-relationships-phone-email/

to do that. Emails can have the additional benefit that it makes it easy for the customer to forward your information to their colleagues. That allows YOU to communicate directly with the other decision makers and influencers, rather than your customer.

However, don't be fooled. Communicating the technical information is NOT the most important thing to accomplish.

You've heard it before… "People buy from people they like." "People buy for emotional reasons."

If it's appropriate, reply to the email by suggesting some times for a phone conversation rather than answering the questions via email. At a minimum, use your email to tee up your next call. "I've attached the technical specifications that you asked for. There's a lot here and I know you're busy. Let's talk for 15 minutes so that I can highlight 2 or 3 of the essential elements I know you'll want to review based on our earlier conversation."

It's true that some customers are super busy and would rather communicate via email, text message, etc. Always keep in mind that there is a declining scale of "emotional bond" established or nurtured in various forms of communication.

Is Your Communication Personal?

#1 - Face to face communication

#2 - Webcam meeting

#3 - Phone call

#4 - Written conversation

When you're forced to use written conversation, be sure to "overcompensate" and ask about the personal stuff at the opening of the email and then get down to business.

By focusing your attention on the customer during calls and maintaining your attention, you'll build a stronger sense of the customer and will have a much better intuitive feel for what the best way to nurture the relationship is at each step along the way.

3 Phone Mistake - Speed

One thing that most salespeople get wrong in inbound sales models is initial contact. Fast response is the name of the game.

Companies and salespeople are not generally very good at lead follow up in the first place. A Forbes article of 2012[9] stated that 36% of inbound leads are never called at all.

Many studies show that the odds of success drop from 75% to less than 5% within 15 minutes of a lead "converting" or calling in.

For that reason, it's crucial that leads are distributed to salespeople automatically and instantly and contingency plans made so that if a salesperson responsible for a given territory or product line is unavailable, someone else on the team can make the call.

Salespeople should see quick response to leads as a top priority. The result will be higher qualification rates for leads, higher ROI on advertising and marketing and fewer leads that slip through the cracks and never get a call.

4 Phone Mistake - All Leads are the Same

Understanding the quality of inbound leads is crucial. There may be various marketing campaigns generating leads and the quality of those leads can vary widely. A lead that filled out a form in order to get a report or whitepaper is not at the Purchase phase. A customer that decides to start a Free Trial could be ready to purchase but, is probably not. The salesperson has to be able to categorize the incoming leads and provide each lead with the information they need given their place in the process and follow up to help them get to the next phase.

Asking questions that identify the position of the customer within their buying process, as discussed in a previous chapter, is essential.

---

9   http://www.forbes.com/sites/kenkrogue/2012/07/27/the-great-marketingsales-disconnect-industry-study-reveals-36-of-leads-never-called/#4e18b22c3808

Salespeople naturally want to move customers to purchasing as quickly as possible and tend to treat every lead as if they're ready to buy now.

In a world where your competitor is only a quick click or two away, it's a mistake to try to close a customer who is just trying to learn about options.

Map out essential questions to identify the customer's place in the buying process and appropriate next steps and collateral that will help the customer stay engaged with your company and move forward in the process to the next step, not all the way to the close.

Funnel Math

Whatever your marketing and sales processes, it's crucial to understand the math behind the process. The cliche, "Sales is a numbers game." is true. Sales performance is ultimately measured in actual sales numbers but, the meaning of the cliche is different. Winning at sales is about understanding the other numbers that drive sales results and keeping your focus on performing there.

What are the actions that lead to sales? Sales processes differ and so will the key sales actions and metrics. However, the two indisputably greatest sources of failure for salespeople are Prospecting and Follow up.

In a completely inbound sales process, there may be no need for either of these. However, it's important for the salesperson to be aware of the importance of these factors in any case. Things change in business all the time for many reasons. A salesperson that is dependent on marketing to generation inbound leads, provide engaging content and other key assets on the website, etc. must know that any change to those elements could have a direct effect on their own results. Of course, if significant changes are made to the marketing mix or messaging and you detect a slowdown in inbound leads or a marked change in the "quality" of the leads, you should have a plan B. Of course, bringing the issue up to management, etc. is important too so you can quickly bounce back. . However, this can often lead to frustration. The business probably has a longer time horizon to see if the changes will really work than the salesperson can see. A salesperson is concerned about their commission check next month. The business may be expecting a slow down this quarter and gains to come further down the road. Will talk more about Plan B later.

In most sales organizations, the salesperson has a responsibility to generate their own leads in one way or another. And this is perennially where things break. It's a natural consequence of human nature. Just like knowing that your tend to have a led foot on the open freeway allows you to learn to use cruise control to stay out of the patrol car's sights, knowing that you're going to lose focus on prospecting is the first and most important step.

Why does this happen so often? On the one hand, prospecting - finding new people interested in your products and services - is the hardest part of the job and fraught with the most rejection. On the other hand, working with interested customers who you've established a strong relationship with, doing presentations, proposals and getting the order are what salespeople tend to love. So, the natural course of things is that salespeople stay focused on taking care of customers that are well into the process and getting closer and closer to buying and put prospecting off as it doesn't have the same level of "urgency".

But, prospecting is MORE important than closing. If the early phases of the process are managed well, the customer doesn't really need "closing". Ultimately, the customer is in charge of deciding to buy. No salesperson, no matter how good, can make a customer purchase. And things happen out of the salesperson's control to cause even the hottest lead on the planet to stop or choose another alternative. The primary lever the salesperson has in the process that they have full control over is how much effort put into putting new leads into the process.

In a typical sales process, the measurable steps in the process are:

- Outbound Calls to Potential New Leads (people we haven't talked to before)
- Conversations with these Potential New Leads
- New Leads Qualified - meet some minimal criteria to indicate probable need
- Budget and Authority Identified
- Discovery Meetings, Presentations, Demonstrations, Site Visits, etc.
- Proposals

Funnel Math

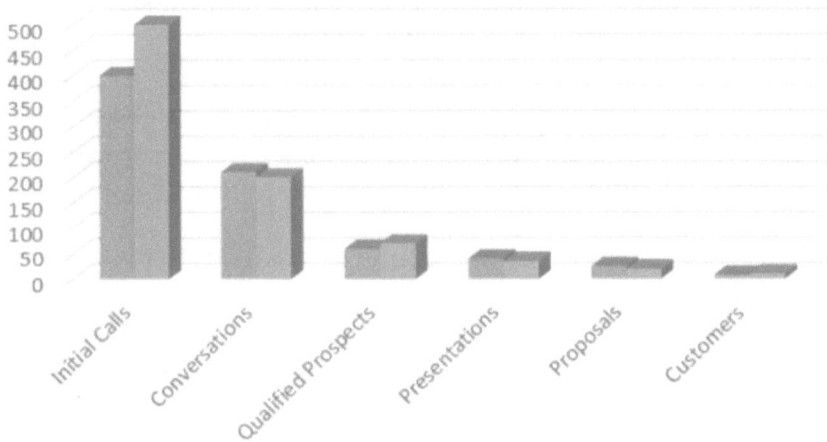

In every business, there are historical or average rates at which leads move from one of these steps to the next. The inability to measure and manage these rates is the undoing of thousands of businesses and millions of salespeople.

The only way to know with any confidence what you'll sell at the end of the month, next month or next quarter is to know how many leads you called, qualified and so on this month, last month or last quarter. Keeping the beginning of the funnel full means the numbers will be there in the end.

The rates shown here are typical across all sorts of businesses. Each business will vary significantly. Use these rates to benchmark your prospecting performance. Did you call enough new leads to generate enough sales last month or this month? If you're not measuring each of these steps, then start. If you don't have a CRM or other automated way to track things, don't wait for that. Just start keeping notes each day and spend an hour each week adding things up.

Play around with these rates and your process and you'll begin to get a sense of how crucial focus on the beginning of the process, the "top of the funnel" is. Here's an example:

If a salesperson wants to double sales, they could choose to change their pricing, terms, contracts, proposal method or even the product itself in hopes that a greater percentage of proposals turn into purchases. This would involve every facet of the business being involved in discussions, decisions and planning and could take considerable time to implement and realize results. As we've touched on before, often when a customer doesn't buy, it has nothing to do with the salesperson or their business. So, there is a natural limit to how high your "close rate" can get. Could it go from 33% to 66%? Maybe but, it would take time and then entire organization would have to be focused on it.

Or, a salesperson can simply make time to reach out to twice as many new prospects, without the need for any other changes, and presto, sales double! Yes, it really is that easy. Can a typical salesperson find the time in their day to make 2x as many prospecting calls? Yes. When you really look at how much time is actually spent calling new leads, it doesn't take a lot of additional time. It just takes focus. Block off windows of time for new lead prospecting calls only. No other distractions. Turn off email. Close the door. Cut down on water cooler time. Skip the HR presentation on the new 401k. Take a shorter lunch break. Come in early and stay late. It's these kinds of little things that separate top producers from everyone else.

The challenge for salespeople in inbound sales processes is that the quality of the leads will vary greatly, often for reasons the salesperson has very limited visibility into. This is another reason that gauging the current phase of the buyer and ensuring their experience in the sales process and via marketing messages is appropriate to their individual phase is crucial.

In an inbound process, the lever that quickly changes results throughout the funnel is still at the top of the funnel but, it's not typically within the salesperson's purview. Visits to the website, online ad impressions and search rankings are often what drive the top of the funnel in this type of process. Salespeople should be kept informed of these metrics as well.

Inbound marketing also has a tendency to attract buyers that want an online experience, sometimes exclusively. In other words, they may not want to talk to a salesperson at all. They may also be using false information, etc. So, there will typically be a far lower rate of real conversations and often a lower rate of qualification of those that do have a conversation.

Plan B - What to do when things are slowing down.

In an outbound sales process, when things slow down it's most often a lack of outbound calling or networking or referrals or whatever your typical "top of the funnel" activity is. Tracking and measuring the things discussed above will show you that. If initial calls are lower than average, then everything else will be lower too. The solution is to ramp up outbound lead generation activity.

In an inbound sales process, then reduced inbound leads is the first place to look. Ramp up ad spending, email marketing and other activities that typically drive inbound leads.

However, if you see that your initial calls or inbound leads are on par with normal, then identify the stage or step where things drop off most significantly and focus there. Why has the rate of people that go from qualified to presentation dropped off? Is there a new offering in the market that is more appealing to them? Do you need to answer that in your approach or packages?

From Ideas to Practice

I have personally read hundreds of books on selling, and I am assuming this is not the first that you have read. Some ideas I've adopted and put into practice quickly, while some have taken me years to grasp and refine.

Experience tells me that the key to making forward progress is to be reasonable in your expectations of yourself and your sales team. Don't try to change everything at once. Pick 2 or 3 ideas of processes that you feel will have the biggest impact on results. Focus on getting those changes in place first, and move on to more only after you and the team are all in agreement that the changes you've made are having a positive impact.

You're all busy doing what you do the way you do it. Changing your sales processes and approaches with customers is like changing the tires on a moving vehicle. Change one at a time! Give yourself and your team time to adjust and adapt, don't expect everyone to get it right in the first few days.

Leadership

The first ingredient is for your team to know that you're serious about the changes you're making. The message cannot be "Here are some interesting ideas. Let's try them out and see what happens." That will fail. The message has to be "I've learned about some new approaches and I want to implement a few of them carefully. Here's how I think they'll benefit our business, you as salespeople and our customers. Here's what I'd like to start doing, and here's how we'll measure that."

In fact, if you can offer some sort of incentive or reward for those that adapt quickly is a great way to motivate your team. It's also a great idea to include some or all of the team in building and working through the plan of action.

If you haven't been measuring sales activity at all, instead of measuring how many calls to new leads were made this week immediately, start by measuring how many salespeople submit their call activity on time and completely the first few weeks. Provide help to those that don't.

Once everyone on the team is trying to follow the new processes and procedures and providing the expected information, then start measuring the depth of knowledge about the customer. In the end, does it matter how many times the phone gets dialed or how much you learn about the customers and their needs?

Track what key details have been learned and grade accounts and salespeople based on the completeness of your knowledge about those customers. This will focus salespeople on building relationships, asking great questions and listening rather than leaving lots of voicemails.

I believe the key to success in building a world class sales team is by giving people freedom to follow their instincts while focusing on the end goal. In the end, any salesperson's goal must be to know the customer's needs as intimately as possible and to fulfill those needs if possible.

In this type of environment, some salespeople will come up with creative ways to leverage technology or even use "old school" techniques to find success, which all of your team can benefit from. This creates a culture of innovation and improvement that people enjoy.

Managing salespeople is difficult. Keeping them motivated is one of the most difficult challenges. Avoid creating an environment that makes them feel micro-managed. Create a culture that recognizes that deep relationships with customers in your market have long term value, and that this is just as important as closing sales.

About the Author

https://twitter.com/craigklein

https://www.linkedin.com/in/kleincraig

https://salesnexus.com/blog/

Craig is the founder and CEO of SalesNexus.com, a leading web based CRM, marketing automation and lead generation solution for sales teams from 10 to 100. Craig works with small startups and Fortune 500's to create systems that give salespeople more time to sell and more quality leads to sell to, while giving management the accountability that is so elusive in sales.

Prior to founding SalesNexus, Craig spent 15 years building and leading sales teams selling multi-million dollar, multi-year contracts to energy companies such as ExxonMobil, BP, Shell and Chevron. The long, complex selling environment within these energy behemoths gives Craig a keen sense of the risk of mis-allocated sales time.

Craig's superior ability to discern a business owner's goals, challenges and needs stems from his strong belief that listening skills are far more valuable than speaking skills. Craig's belief that business growth is the engine of human advancement has led him to co-found SalesGrowthHub.com and to serve as a mentor to students in the University of Houston's Wolff Center for Entrepreneurship.

Craig has written several popular e-books including "Grow Sales with Emails – 7 Simple Steps Salespeople Can Take Today"[10] and the recent "Email Marketing for Sales Teams - Best Practices".[11] Craig is a contributor to Small Business Today Magazine, Premier Agent Magazine, The Customer Collective and SocialMediaToday.com. He has appeared as a featured speaker at the Digital Marketer's Email World 2013,[12] TEANA 2012 Conference, the American Association of Inside Sales Professionals Executive Summit 2015 and many other exhibitions and conferences.

Craig's the father of 3 beautiful children. He's an avid sailor, hunter and skier. When he's not growing SalesNexus or writing, he's probably planning his next adventure to somewhere you've never heard of.

---

10   http://salesgrowthhub.com/grow-sales-with-emails-ebook/
11   https://salesnexus.com/blog/email-marketing-sales-teams-best-practices/
12   http://www.salesnexus.com/blog/craig-klein-speaks-at-email-world

Special Offer

If what you've read here has inspired you to take things to the next level, we want to help! The following are some free and easy ways to learn more and take the next steps in building your future -

Learn the art of practicing the principles in this book.
Join our Inside-Out Selling Webinar:
https://salesnexus.com/webinar.html

Measure and Manage Sales, Generate Leads and Nurture Leads

Start a Free Trial of SalesNexus:
https://logon.salesnexus.com/gettingstarted/step1.aspx

Learn to generate leads and turn cold leads into hot ones - Download "Email Marketing for Sales Teams, Best Practices":
https://salesnexus.com/blog/email-marketing-sales-teams-best-practices/

www.ingramcontent.com/pod-product-compliance
Lightning Source LLC
Chambersburg PA
CBHW020710180526
45163CB00008B/3019